ARMOURBEARER

Wife

LISA MAKI

Dedication

I dedicate this book, first and foremost, to my Father, my Abba who created me. Thank you for all your chastening and discipline. Thank you for your confidence in me. Thank you for everything you taught me through my trials.

To my husband, Jason Maki, this book would not have been possible if I didn't have you in my life. My being your wife has been the most challenging but rewarding experience I have ever had. Thank you for your great love and for the best friendship anyone can ever offer me.

To my dear little sister, April Christian: This book is for you. God connected us at the most perfect time. You are a living witness to my transition to an Armour-Bearer wife. Thank you for your friendship and for the laughter. You are such a source of joy. You are definitely an Armour-Bearer wife in the making.

To my friend and sister from London, Jacqueline Ani: Isn't it amazing how God connected us, only for us to go through the same marital trials at almost the same time, and gain victory also at the same time? What we learned during our trials is what really connected our souls and spirits. Thank you for all your encouragement and for the time you spent ministering to me and reminding me of my calling.

To Jasmine Andrews: You are another Facebook sister and friend who God connected to me at the most perfect time. Thank you for sharing with me about conquering demonic kings. You are a crucial part of the Armour-Bearer Wife group.

To all the other members of the Armour-Bearer Wife Facebook group: Ronessa, Risa, Jessica, Fedena, Killairay, and the rest of you: You are a great source of encouragement to me. Keep fighting the good fight. I am looking forward to hearing more breakthroughs!

To all my other fellow wives who have embraced, are beginning to embrace, and who will embrace their calling as Armour-Bearers to their husbands: this book is for you.

Contents

Preface

This book is only for wives who are willing to fight for their marriage. It is for wives who believe in Jesus/Yeshua and the power of His Word. If you are single but you want to learn about being an Armour-Bearer wife, then this book is also for you. If you are not a believer of Jesus but you are tired of your marital problems and want to make your marriage work out, this book will open your eyes to another dimension. Though this book was not written for men, they are not banned from reading it. So if you are a man wanting to read this book, let me warn you that you will see another side of the woman that you probably have not seen at any time in your life – the woman warrior that God created her to be.

Prologue

Now Jesus was teaching in one of the synagogues on the Sabbath. And there was a woman who for eighteen years had had an illness caused by a spirit (demon). She was bent double, and could not straighten up at all. When Jesus saw her, He called her over and said to her, "Woman, you are released from your illness." Then He laid His hands on her; and immediately she stood erect again and she began glorifying and praising God (Luke 13:10-13, The Amplified Bible).

I was in my quiet time early one morning when the Holy Spirit gave me this Scripture. Two things caught my attention: the 18 years and the illness caused by a spirit (demon). I looked back and tried to remember what happened to me 18 years ago. It was the time when I separated from my ex husband and the time when I got seriously involved with a married man. I then realized that God was pointing back to "18 years ago" as the root source of a lot of my issues. As to the demonic spirit causing it, I didn't think much about it at that time. Since the Scripture says: "Woman, you are released from your illness", I took it to mean that God was reminding me that I am already healed.

What I failed to understand then was that God was declaring the end from the beginning. He was showing me an end result to what He was going to do to me for the next months after that. Isn't our God tricky in a holy way? I mean, He knew that had He told me that I was going to go through something that will really test me, I would have probably ran away and said, "no way" (as if I can run away from Him though). Thus was the start of my journey into the Armour-Bearer role.

The days, weeks, and months that followed surely tested me in ways that couldn't have happened in any other situation. Everything I have learned, applied, relearned, and reapplied is all in this book.

I saw with my own eyes how the spiritual manifested into the physical. I saw demonic spirits fleeing. I saw things change drastically.

However, the enemy taunted me. The more I persisted, the more stubborn he became. The more I worked in rebuilding the walls, the more furious he became. It was a replica of the story of Nehemiah when Tobiah and Sanballat were harassing him during the rebuilding of the temple. And just as Nehemiah became more determined to finish the work that he started, I was unwavering in my efforts to finish rebuilding the walls, which includes the writing of this book.

I needed one more thing ... one last thing, and that was a breakthrough. I told God that I didn't care whether I receive my breakthrough in the physical realm because I already saw it in the spiritual realm. However, others need to see that what the Holy Spirit taught me actually works. I needed an actual testimony to prove that everything in this book is tried and tested. I finally had my breakthrough.

This book is not meant to be read like a novel. You need to set aside a place and time to read it ... just you and God without any distractions. You need a journal or notebook to do the workshops. If you take this seriously, you will win the battle.

Introduction

You are not reading this by chance. You have probably reached the end of the line but you are giving yourself one last hope – something that can probably help you regain strength. Perhaps you have prayed all the prayers you can think of and you don't even know what to pray for anymore. You are just tired! But you do not want to give up just yet.

Let me tell you something. This book would not have even come to my mind had it not been for that same situation you are in. I know how it's like to feel so tired in the marriage. I know how it's like to doubt whether your marriage is even from God or not. Believe me … I have been where you are, maybe not in exactly the same way but the same circumstances, the same feelings, the same doubts, the same fears.

What I want you to bear in mind is that you are not going through your problems simply to go through it. God is not punishing you or putting you to the test just because He wants to. He is building your character, so you can be conformed to the image and likeness of His Son, Jesus Christ. Isn't this the whole purpose of salvation? It is not just for us to go to heaven but for us to

13

be "like Jesus". In fact, Jesus Himself said in John 17:3 that *"eternal life is knowing God"*. The word "know" in this text is synonymous to how a man knows his wife. The husband and wife become "one" through knowing each other.

Your trials in your marriage are meant for you to become more "one" with Jesus. You become "one" with Him through your sufferings. You become "one" with Him through the character that God is building in you.

What wives seem to forget is that their marriage is an extension of their walk with God. Every instruction of God should be applied in marriage – laying down your life for your brother, denying yourself, loving others, turning the other cheek, and so on and so forth. Unfortunately, this is not the case most of the time. The wife complains that she doesn't have any right in the marriage … that her husband does not know how to listen to her … that her husband does not care about how she feels. She loses track of "the call". The focus turns to the self and before long she is drowning in her emotions, which is exactly what the devil wants to happen.

Women, your emotions can be your biggest enemy. It can be the greatest hindrance to deliverance, healing, and the fulfillment of God's vision – both for you and your husband, respectively and as a couple. Your emotions can blind you from seeing what is really going on in the spiritual realm. Your emotions can make you see your husband as your enemy. Your emotions can make you give up on your marriage and make the devil gain the victory.

This book is meant to awaken you to the spiritual reality of your situation. It will help you develop your godly emotions, which are the fruits of the Holy Spirit. It will teach you to heighten your spiritual discernment so you can fight the battle more strategically. It will strengthen you in ways you have never imagined you could.

This book is not meant to be read quickly. I suggest you pause after every chapter and do the workshop. My goal is to guide you step by step, in very precise and strategic ways. Remember, we are not warring against flesh and blood but against principalities of darkness.

I now welcome you to the best training you will ever go through as a wife.

Lisa Maki

Opening Prayer

Heavenly Father. You know why I am reading this book. You know why I need this book. Nothing about me is hidden from you. You know my down sitting and my uprising. You know my thoughts from afar. You are very familiar with every fiber of my being.

As I begin to open the pages and read each chapter of this book, I ask that you speak clearly to me. Let your Holy Spirit lead and guide me accordingly. Quicken my spirit and let every word I will hear be the words that I need to hear, not only the words that I want to hear.

I bind every spirit that will hinder or distract me from reading or understanding your message — spirits of laziness, stubbornness, tiredness, busyness, resistance, disobedience, depression, anxiety, and distrust (continue mentioning spirits you discern). In the name of Jesus, I bind these hindering spirits. I loose the spirits of submission, excitement for your word, obedience, joy, and trust, in Jesus' name.

I humbly ask for forgiveness for any sin in me that I have not repented for. Forgive me for (confess your sins). I release any anger or unforgiveness I feel towards my husband. I receive your spirit of peace.

Speak to me, Father. I'm listening. In Jesus' name, AMEN!

Lisa Maki

CHAPTER 1

The Wife, The Armour Bearer

What I will share with you will change your view of your role as a wife, and marriage in general. It will make you see that most of your problems are not what they seem to be. It will make you realize that your husband is not your enemy; the devil is!

It was a few years back when a Prophet's wife shared with me that she is her husband's armour-bearer. At that time, I've only heard of the word "armour-bearer" a few times in my walk as a believer of Yeshua, but never as a wife's role. The more I grew in my marriage, the more I realized how true this role is for us, wives.

According to Dictionary.com, an armour-bearer is "an officer selected by kings and generals because of his bravery, not only to bear their armour, but also to stand by them in the time of danger."

Another definition of an armour-bearer that I found is "one who helps, a helper, to give strength, support." Honestly, this is more like the role of a wife and help-meet, which clearly explains our role as "armour-bearers".

In short, as an armour-bearer of my husband, my role is to protect him in the time of danger. I believe that this includes my ability to discern danger before it hits, to give me a better chance of protecting him. This, I believe, is the reason why wives have the ability to smell danger from afar. God did not give us this gift for nothing.

Before I proceed, I want you to drop all your preconceived notions about marriage and your expectations from your husbands. I want you to lay down your fleshly emotions – your hurts, anger, frustrations, anxieties, and fears with regards to your marriage. Drop all these down and imagine yourself as a Warrior Queen, an armour-bearer of the King.

Now imagine that a host of army is about to attack your King and you see it miles away. You can't tell him because you have to protect him and your Kingdom. Telling him may make him rush to the war zone and get killed. You now prepare for battle and put on your whole armour. You grab your sword, put it on its sheath, and you get your shield. You ride your horse and proceed to attack the enemies of your Kingdom.

Does this look like some desperate, crying, anxious, fearful, depressed wife to you? Does this look like a wife who is complaining about her husband – that she is not receiving love from him ... that he is cheating on her ... that he is not treating her right ... that he is not responsible ... etc. etc.? NOT AT ALL!!! This Warrior Queen knows her role and is detached from all the worldly emotions that can consume her and therefore jeopardize her Kingdom.

You can be this Warrior Queen. God has already equipped you to be one. He has provided you with all the armour you need. He has given you a King and a Kingdom to fight for and protect.

Do you now realize why the devil is taunting us with our emotions? He wants to cripple us and paralyze us so we can't fight for our husbands and our families. Satan knows our power as armour-bearers. Why do you think did he attack Eve first? He could have tempted Adam, but nope ... he chose Eve. And when he got Eve, he got Adam as well.

Workshop 1

Answer the following questions as honestly as you can. Do not rush. Take time meditating and answering each question. Ask the Holy Spirit to guide you.

1. What emotions are weighing you down concerning your husband and marriage?
2. Why are you feeling this way?
3. When did these feelings start?

The emotions you just wrote down that are weighing you down are the devil's most powerful weapons against you. Where all these feelings started are the root issues that may even be deeper than that. This is what God is purging you from. Keep reading and you will see things clearly.

The devil loves to whisper in our ears: *he doesn't care about you … he doesn't even love you so why submit to him? … he is going to hurt you again, it is not safe … he is not satisfied with you … he finds that other girl hotter … he can't even provide for you.*

It doesn't take a minute to make us listen to that voice and start believing it. Before long we are operating in the lie more than the truth. We cry out to God and nothing is happening. We cast out all spirits of lust, pride, and control, and it is still there. You know why? I will tell you two reasons why.

The first reason is our own underlying issues. In fact, the negative feelings we have towards our husbands are merely reflections of our own issues that God is still dealing with. Unless we see things this way, we will never be able to heal from these issues that are getting in the way of winning our battles in our marriage. Go back to the "emotions that are weighing you down" that you wrote, and ask God to expose to you the underlying issues. As you continue to read this book, you will also experience healing and deliverance. What is important for now is that you are aware of these issues and are obeying God in the steps you need to take.

The second reason is something I've learned from someone recently ... someone I don't even know but who God has used time and time again to give me very timely messages.

This person shared with me that if our shield has holes, we can't use it effectively. The holes are fears and doubts we have entertained. To patch up these holes require the Word of God. In fact, this person said that the entire shield is made up of the Word of God.

Our sword is the Word and our faith is the shield. We may have a very powerful sword but if our shield is not solid, then we will falter. Thus, as armour-bearers, we have to make sure that our shield is intact.

The enemy is not our husbands. The battle is not won through arguments and even discussions. The enemy is the devil and the battle is won in the presence of God.

Now imagine yourself again as the Warrior Queen and you are going to face and confront one of the biggest enemies of your Kingdom (your marriage and family). It may be the spirit of a cheating husband, an abusive husband, a husband addicted to porn, a drug-addicted husband, a husband bound to alcohol, a lazy husband, etc. Remember, you are warring against spirits here. You are getting ready for the battle. You get your sword, which is the Bible, and you polish it by meditating on it and even writing down the ones that talk about your victory. You slowly walk into the battlefield with your sword and shield, and with the helmet of salvation, belt of truth, breastplate of righteousness, and the gospel of peace on your feet. You begin to war by worshipping God and declaring all the promises He has given you.

You continue warring through praise and worship, thanking God for His faithfulness. The war continues and escalates as you begin to smash all the lies of the enemy, replacing each lie with the truth. You shield your husband by interceding for him and breaking down strongholds. Finally, you go back and continue to worship and praise God as your enemies lay before you dead and defeated.

This is our role, my fellow wives and sisters in Yeshua. And if this is our mindset and understanding, we will continue to win, no matter how difficult it gets. Don't forget that as armour-bearers we are to take the bullet for our husbands, in the same way that Yeshua died for us.

One last thing that I want to share with you is a Scripture I saw, which is the very reason why I started writing this. It is in 1 Samuel 31 where King Saul was talking to his armour-bearer.

He said: *"Draw your sword and thrust me through. Otherwise my enemies will come, run me through, and make a sport of me."*

Let me paraphrase this based on the revelation that the Holy Spirit gave me. Think of it as your husband talking to you.

"My beloved wife, my armour-bearer; draw your sword, the Word of God, and thrust it into my soul. Otherwise the devil will thrust his sword into my soul and make fun of me."

Our problems with our husbands are just the tip of the iceberg. The underlying issues run deep. These problems are meant for us to hear an inner groaning of their spirits to be released from whatever the enemy is holding against them – generational curses, bondages, strongholds, past issues. They are crying out to us without them even knowing it. They are asking us to fight for them in the spiritual realm, to draw our sword and finally thrust this Word deep into their soul.

This is how we will win all our battles in our marriage, my fellow Armour-Bearers.

The Qualifications of an Armour Bearer Wife

Yes you were created to be an Armour-Bearer wife; but unless you sign up for it, you will never be one. You can't just sign up though unless you believe you are qualified. Below are the qualifications of an Armour-Bearer wife.

✓ Must have or willing to have a consistent daily quiet time alone with God (at least 30 minutes for beginners) in worship, prayer, and study of the Word.

✓ Must be serious in saving her marriage, no matter what happens.

✓ Must be submitted to God's command of submission to the husband.

✓ Must have a gentle and quiet spirit.

✓ Must be willing to fast and go into deep intercession and warfare prayer.

If you have these qualifications, or at least have the serious willingness to do all these, you are ready to proceed to the next chapters and harness your Armour-Bearer Wife qualities.

CHAPTER 2

The Queen, the Armour-Bearer

Think of the queen in a chess game. She is the most powerful piece, able to move any number of squares vertically, horizontally, or diagonally. She protects the king like no other piece in the game. Having the most moves, she can be the most used among all the other pieces. She multitasks between guarding the king, fighting the enemies, and working with other members.

So many Christian wives are clueless as to how powerful the role of a wife is, more so her role as an Armour-Bearer. Women connote power with success, and sadly, even their ability to make their husbands follow what they want. Each time you mention having a "gentle and quiet" spirit as a requirement for being a wife, there is always an uproar, resistance, or rebellion. Very few have a good grasp of the power of the queen, just like this piece in the chess game.

This queen in the chess game is not some pampered wife who gets what she wants; neither is she a scared, crying, depressed wife who feels the weight of the world on her shoulders. She knows her role and is confident about it.

This queen is not dependent on the king for her moves. She knows her position even without the king telling her what to do. She is not relying on the king for approval for her to feel good about herself. She knows what she is called to do and she does it to the best of her ability.

You were created as a queen, which is why you have a king. The devil knows this fully well, which is why he doesn't even want you to understand your role. Believe me, just writing this book was a big threat to the enemy. He has been trying to kill this baby before it was even born. He knows that once this book is released, women will be awakened, and a new kind of "Queenship" will emerge.

This Queenship is not about control but about humility; it is not about physical or material power but spiritual power; it is not about reigning but about surrendering.

CHAPTER 3

Jesus, our Armour-Bearer

It is amazing how 1 Peter 3 begins with: *In the same way, you wives, submit to your husbands*. The phrase: "in the same way" refers to something that we should pattern our submission to. Let us go backwards a few verses, in the previous chapter.

When He was insulted, He didn't retaliate with insults; when He suffered, He didn't threaten, but handed them over to Him who judges justly. He himself bore our sins in his body on the stake, so that we might die to sins and live for righteousness — by His wounds you were healed (1 Peter 2:23-24).

Do you realize my fellow wives that we are asked to submit to our husbands the way Jesus submitted to the perfect will of the Father? This is not about being controlled or stepped on but humbling ourselves and trusting God. Let's go back to that Scripture again to understand what submission really is.

When He was insulted, He didn't retaliate with insults. How many times have you felt that your husband insulted you? How did you feel? Did you talk back at him? Did you insult him as well? I can't begin to tell you how many times I've felt insulted by my own husband. At one point I punched the wall out of anger. Praise God I didn't break my hand. What would Jesus do? What did Jesus do? *He didn't retaliate with insults.* Jesus had the power to freeze anyone who insulted him and turn him into stone. I don't know what I would have done if I had Jesus' power. My husband would have turned into a statue a long time ago.

When He suffered, He didn't threaten, but handed them over to Him who judges justly. How many times have you threatened to leave or divorce your husband in the midst of your suffering? How many times did you fight back to defend yourself? I have walked away from my husband a few times, and even left him for a few months, without him knowing where I was. This was definitely not the way Jesus wanted me to handle it. This was not His way.

You can say, "But that's not fair. You mean God just wants me to shut up? Does God want me to get hurt and suffer?" You want to know the truth? God is more concerned about our holiness than our happiness. The essence of our salvation is to be conformed to the image

32

and likeness of Jesus, not to live happily ever after. In fact, the Bible says that God chastens those He loves.

God does not want us to suffer and leave us there. He is telling us to hand over our suffering to Him because He knows best. It is all about trusting in Him. This is easier said than done, really. Yet when we begin to see the bigger picture, it becomes easier.

He himself bore our sins in his body on the stake, so that we might die to sins and live for righteousness — by His wounds you were healed. This is the part in "1 Peter 2" that hit me the most, and which made me understand why God is telling us to submit the way Jesus did. *Jesus bore our sins in his body so we might die to sins and live for righteousness.* Do you see how *not retaliating when insulted,* and *not threatening when going through suffering* can deliver your husband? Let me explain this more clearly.

Your husband's anger, bad behavior, unjust ways, immoral acts, and anything evil in him is rooted deep down inside of him. It may have come from his parents, how he was treated, his hurts, and the abuse he has been through. In short, what he is manifesting to you that hurts you is an indicator of what is going on inside of him that he has to heal from. Each time he lashes out on you, you become like Jesus who bore our sins ... if you choose to do it the way Jesus did. *By His wounds you were*

33

healed. Through your wounds, your husband will be healed.

If it is getting hard for you to receive this message, I suggest you stop reading and spend some time alone with God. Ask Him to show you what is going on with you, and why it is hard to accept this submission part in Scripture. Believe me, it took me a long time before I finally understood. And if I don't examine myself every so often, I can easily fall back to where I was. However, if you see the depth of this message, it will totally change your concept of submission, and will change your marriage too.

You are a catalyst to your husband's healing and deliverance ... but only if you submit the way Jesus did.

Tell me ... did Jesus' submission make Him lesser or greater? Greater of course! This is what being an Armour-Bearer is. Jesus is the greatest Armour-Bearer.

CHAPTER 4

Her Biggest Stronghold

Now that you realize the greater significance of being an Armour-Bearer wife, the next step is to fulfill this role. This is where the challenge begins.

There are two sides to warring in the spirit for our marriage: our husband's strongholds that we need to destroy, and our very own strongholds that we may not even be aware of.

According to greatbiblestudy.com, a stronghold is a faulty thinking pattern based on lies and deception. The same source says that deception is one of the primary weapons of the devil, because it is the building blocks for a stronghold.[1]

An example of a stronghold stems from being physically abused in a previous relationship. The thinking pattern that may have developed is a defensive mindset, to protect oneself from being hurt again. This may lead the woman to think that her husband is attacking her,

---

[1] Strongholds (http://www.greatbiblestudy.com/strongholds.php) 2008

even if he is not. It may lead her to run away from the marriage when he is raising his voice, thinking that he is getting mad and will hurt her. Another example comes from being cheated on in a previous relationship. This was my stronghold. It developed in me a thick wall that refused to be close to any man emotionally. I associated emotional closeness and love to getting hurt.

Until we subdue and kill our own strongholds, we will not win this battle. We won't be able to fight or intercede for our marriage and husbands.

Our husband's strongholds may even stir up the very strongholds that we have, hindering us from being able to even enter the battlefield. For instance, if you have major insecurity issues and your husband's stronghold is lust, then that will be a big problem for you. Instead of being able to war for him in the spiritual realm, you will be sucked into your insecurities and end up being depressed, angry, and hurt.

Only God can expose to us our strongholds, which normally come to the surface during severe trials. Job 36:8-10 says: *"If, then, they are bound in chains, held in oppressive cords, He shows them the results of their doings ... He sounds a warning in their ears ...*

I knew that I had issues with control but didn't realize how bad it was until I faced one of my biggest battles in my marriage. I grew up with a dad who didn't express his love for me. My hunger for his attention made me rebel against him. The only way he knew how to handle my rebellion was to control me. However, the more he controlled me, the more I rebelled against him. My fear of being controlled made me the kind of person who wanted to always be in control of every situation. I also became very defensive; when I sensed control, I took over or ran away.

This fear of control made me: attack my husband a few times; rebel against him; and run away from him.

During the first year of my marriage, I was so enraged with my husband that I ran towards him like a bull, jumped on him, and bit his hand. I never knew I had that strength in me. I am barely 5 feet tall and small-framed, while my husband is 6 feet. He could hardly believe what I did. I was pretty shocked myself. That bite left a snake-bite mark on his hand which really scared me. It was like God showing me that it was the spirit of the enemy that jumped on me.

How can a woman of God who was already a leader in ministry do something like that? How can a woman who was so intimate with Jesus be filled with so much rage? The answer lies in her "strongholds" that God began to expose at that time.

I've had several fights with my husband where it got worse because I didn't buckle down. The worst fight I had with him was when I felt that he was really the devil. The more I resisted him, the more powerful the evil spirit in him became. It made me very weary and discouraged. I left as a result. What I didn't know then that I know now is that my stronghold of "fear of control" fed the stronghold of "control" that he had. I was trying to bind the spirit of control that was in him without realizing that my fear of control was stirring it up. I was fighting flesh with flesh. No wonder I couldn't win.

Workshop 2

I want you to take a break from reading this book and go back to the list of emotions and feelings you wrote down in Workshop 1. Follow my instructions on the list below. Ask the Holy Spirit to guide you step by step.

1. Go back to your past and think of any incident that may have created in you these feelings you wrote

down regarding your marriage. Take away your mind from your husband when doing this.

2. For each story in the past that the Holy Spirit brings you back to, think about the strongholds that are attached to each story or incident.

Now there are different types of strongholds that we, wives, may have including insecurities, jealousy, rejection, bitterness, hunger for attention, etc. God revealed to me, through my experience and through Scripture, that the leader or the "king" of all these strongholds is FEAR.

This FEAR is the most powerful tool of the enemy against us. It is the root cause of all our underlying issues that hinder our effectiveness as Armour-Bearers.

The issue of insecurity is rooted to the fear of being abandoned, hurt, or rejected. The issue of jealousy is rooted to the fear of being betrayed. In short, all our issues are connected to fear – whether it is fear of the future or fear of what happened in the past.

The spirit of fear is an evil spirit that can cripple us and disable us to stand up straight. Without stable and solid legs, we will not be able to perform our role as Armour-Bearers.

Let me bring you to 1 Peter 3:6 to further explain this "king" of our strongholds.

"You are true daughters of Sarah if you do what is right and do not succumb to fear."

"Succumb" means to surrender to something that is powerful. Obviously, it is something powerful enough to be warned not to "surrender" or "give in" to.

The New Living Translation says: *"You are true daughters of Sarah if you do what is right without fear of what your husbands might do."*

This spirit of fear always attacks us in the realm of "what our husbands might do".

What if he chooses that other woman over me? … What if he leaves me? … What if he won't be able to provide for us anymore? … What if he will hurt me again? … What if he goes back to being an alcoholic? … What if he looks at porn? … What if he cheats on me? … What if he wastes our money? … What if he can't find a job? … What if he suffers a heart attack? And so on and so forth.

These fears make us panic, nag our husband, feel insecure, feel suspicious, run away, rebel, and take matters into our own hands. In short, it "gets us in the flesh". This is what the devil wants. If he can get us in the flesh, then we will not win.

We are not warring against flesh and blood, remember? This is not a physical war but a spiritual one. So to win the spiritual war, we have to be in the spirit.

The next question now is: How do we fight this stronghold of fear? How do we conquer this beast?

My answers to this question will blow your mind. Actually, they are not my answers but the answers that the Holy Spirit gave me, which blew my mind.

The mind of our flesh is sense and reason. It is the mind that thinks about logical things such as: "I will leave my husband if he cheats on me." This is very logical. Why will you stay with a man who is cheating on you? The mind of the flesh will never subject itself to the Word of God. It is the mind of our flesh that the devil attacks with fear. And since this mind responds and reacts through sense and reason, then everything the devil will plant in it will sound very logical and reasonable.

To defeat this stronghold of fear is to control the mind *with the spirit and not with the flesh.*

When I began to ask God how to do this, He brought me to Hosea 10:12: *"Break up unused (or uncultivated) ground."*

He then started to show me that the "ground" is the "heart". My spiritual heart is uncultivated and unused. I have to start breaking it. How do I break it?

We are not used to utilizing the heart of the spirit. It is always the heart of the flesh that operates. All our past issues of insecurities, hurts, betrayal, rejection, etc. are rooted in the heart of our flesh. They have become a hardening agent causing us to justify our feelings and actions.

To break the heart of the spirit is to start using it and to begin operating in nothing but what the Word of God says. To break the heart of the spirit is to silence the heart of the flesh when it tries to justify its actions, or find excuses to brush off what God says in His Word.

The heart of the spirit will cling to God's Word that says: I hate divorce. The heart of the flesh will brush that off and say, "but he is cheating on me."

Let me bring you back again to 1 Peter 3 and see further what God says in His Word about our role as wives. Take note of the underlined words.

In the same way, wives, <u>submit to your husbands</u>; so that even if some of them do not believe the Word, <u>they will be won over</u> by your <u>conduct</u>, <u>without your saying anything,</u> 2 as they see your <u>respectful and pure behavior</u>. 3 Your beauty should not *consist in externals such as fancy hairstyles, gold jewelry or what you wear; 4 rather, let it be the inner character of your heart, with the imperishable quality of a <u>gentle and quiet spirit.</u> In God's sight this is of great value. 5 This is how the holy women of the past who put their hope in God used to adorn themselves and submit to their husbands, 6 the way Sarah obeyed Avraham, honoring him as her lord.*

To make my point clearer, I will present a distinction between the heart of flesh and the heart of the spirit based on the verses above.

Heart of Flesh: Why will I submit to my husband if he is not submitted to God?
Heart of Spirit: I will submit to my husband because God says so.

Heart of Flesh: He needs to understand that what he is doing is affecting me badly. He is not getting it!!!
Heart of Spirit: I will continue being the example of Jesus in his life. I will let Jesus' light expose to him what is wrong with him.

Heart of Flesh: How can I respect a man who drinks all day, doesn't have a job, and watches porn?

Heart of Spirit: I respect my husband because God put him above me and because God commanded me to do so.

Heart of Flesh: So you just want me to shut up? We need to communicate.

Heart of Spirit: "Father, I know my husband will not understand no matter how I explain. So I will leave it to you to talk to him."

I can already hear some women saying ... "So you just want me to be a doormat?" This is my response to that: "Well, that devil is already making you a doormat. So what do you do now?"

We all know that it is easier to operate in the heart of flesh. This is our nature! And this is why to operate in the heart of the spirit takes a lot of discipline and self-control, which are actually the fruits of the Spirit. This means that the more we train our hearts to follow our spirits, the more disciplined we will even become; thus, the easier it will get.

And guess what? If you are resisting this and don't want to do it, it's on you. That immediately disqualifies you from the category of ARMOUR-BEARER QUEENS who will reign with Yeshua someday.

1 John 4:18 says: *There is no fear in love ... the person who keeps fearing has not been brought to maturity in regard to love.*

Did you read that? *A person who keeps fearing has not been brought to maturity in regard to love.* Our heart of flesh is so used to the worldly love that focuses on the self. So if you want to mature in love, then you have to train that heart of yours to listen to your spirit.

The very reason why we are even "saved" is so that we can be set apart and be perfected like Yeshua. Training the mind and heart of our spirit is merely a preparation for our eternal life.

It takes a true warrior wife, a real armour-bearer, to be able to break the ground of the heart of the spirit and start operating in it. You know why? Because it is hard! Anything difficult is not for the faint of heart. Remember: NARROW IS THE PATH.

The choice is yours. If you want to defeat the biggest threat to your being an Armour-Bearer wife, then start breaking that uncultivated "heart of the spirit" today.

An Armour-Bearer Queen was attacked by a giant. He was so big and strong; it made the Queen run away and hide. The giant followed her and found her and kept taunting her day and night. Finally, the Queen came out of her hiding place and she began threatening the giant with her sword (the Word of God) while protecting herself with her shield (faith). The more she threatened him with her sword and shield, the smaller he became. Finally, when he became so small, the Queen asked: So what is your name? Who are you? The giant responded with the tiniest voice: "My name is fear."

Lisa Maki

CHAPTER 5

Rebuilding the Walls

You shall be called rebuilder of walls, restorer of homes (Isaiah 58:1).

I t was the most critical time in my marriage when God gave me this Scripture. I was physically separated from my husband then. He went through some major spiritual crisis that made me panic and run away. Yes ... I ran away. And I ran away mad and hurt thinking that I was doing the right thing.

A few months before that incident, I dreamed of a woman I know from Facebook, an intercessor who God connected to me. In my dream she brought me a bouquet of multi-colored flowers. She parked her car and entered through my back door. I told her about my dream and she said that God is calling me to a higher level of intimacy with Him. I kind of brushed off her interpretation at that time. I was so busy with work and making ends meet and I had no extra time for fasting or quiet time with God more than what I already had. Besides, everything seemed okay. We were just getting adjusted to a new home we were renting, after being released from our care giving job for my husband's grandmother.

Looking back to that dream, I now see the symbolisms more clearly. My intercessor friend symbolized the Father. The flowers symbolized love and romance – like God was wooing me to spend more time with Him so He can bring me to a higher level. The multi colors symbolized the brightness and beauty of what is going to take place. The back door symbolized God moving behind me without being noticed, which also explains why it was an unexpected visit.

Had I paid closer attention to the dream and what my friend was saying, things would have not happened the way they did. Instead, I panicked and even made my friend panic. All I saw was some demonic oppression. I tried warring in the spirit but I felt that the demons were so strong. I consulted other people of God without waiting on God to establish divine connections. I talked against my husband and formed alliances with those who were also suspicious of him and his behavior. In short, I gave up and turned over my husband to whatever was trying to take hold of him. I became hurt, bitter, and very rebellious.

It took a while before I realized what I had done. I repented, started picking up the pieces of the mess I made, and reconciled with my husband. Everything started to return to normalcy. I totally forgot about Isaiah 58:1 until God brought it back to my attention by leading me to Scriptures that talk about "rebuilding the walls". It was still not making a lot of sense until the revelation on the Armour-Bearer wife was downloaded by the Holy Spirit to me. Only then did I begin to see deeper and deeper.

Before I go on, let me address one common question I have received from women who read the article: THE WIFE: THE ARMOUR-BEARER from the GodzGurlz web magazine. The question is: "Shouldn't my husband be the one protecting our marriage since he is the head?"

It was a friend of mine, Jacqueline Ani, who explained to me clearly that whoever is stronger spiritually in the marriage should stand in the gap. "Being stronger spiritually", by the way, doesn't have anything to do with titles or positions in ministry. It is one's ability to discern that something is not right, and that there is an attack going on. Your husband may even be a Bishop, but at the time of the attack was not able to see

51

what was about to happen. Remember my dream? That was God's warning to me of something that was about to happen, but which I ignored.

There is a major attack going on in Christian marriages today, more so for those who are big threats to the demonic realm. If you are one of these women who are under severe attack, praise God because it assures you that the devil is scared of you. Strategically, the first person the devil will attack is the head of the marriage, your husband. No matter how spiritually strong your husband is, if the attack is on him then you are expected to stand in the gap. If your husband is not spiritually strong, then all the more should you be like Deborah, leading in the spiritual battle.

So ladies ... let us stop wishing and saying that our husbands should lead. They are already our leaders in the physical realm, technically, because God placed them above us.

The man said, "At last! This is bone from my bones and flesh from my flesh. She is to be called Woman, because she was taken out of Man." This is why a man is to leave his father and mother and stick with his wife, and they are to be <u>one flesh</u> (Genesis 2:23-24).

I never questioned this Scripture until very recently. All of a sudden it dawned on me that it says "one flesh" not "one spirit". I sought God about this and asked the Holy Spirit to give me a revelation.

What was revealed to me was a confirmation to what I previously said … that our husbands are technically our leaders in the "physical" realm. We are "one" with them in the "flesh", meaning in this realm that we are operating in – the realm that we see and feel with our eyes. In this physical realm, we are submitted to them.

Now let's go to the spiritual realm – the realm that we can only see and feel through our spiritual senses. Someday the spiritual and physical will blend and become one; until then, they are separated.

Everything changes in the spiritual realm. There is no husband being above the wife in this realm. It is in this realm where we can take the lead.

The physical realm has its rules, and one of the rules is for us, wives, to submit to our husbands. Another rule is for us to have a gentle and quiet spirit. 2 Timothy 2:5 clearly says that *no athlete wins unless he competes according to the rules.* If we don't follow the rules that God set in His Word for us, wives, we will never win.

The spiritual realm has its set of rules too. One rule is to put on the whole armour of God. Another rule is to walk in the spirit. We can't enter the spiritual realm without being prepared. We can't fight in the spiritual realm without a strategy.

The Strategy

Each of us has a different story. We may have common problems and issues that we are dealing with but the details are still uniquely ours. Your husband is different from mine, and so it follows that my strategy may be different from yours. The bottom line is: You have to create your own strategy. What I am going to present to you are guidelines that you can follow in creating your own personal strategy.

Think of your marriage as a kingdom that the enemy has severely attacked. The walls have been broken, which is the reason why the enemy can just come in and out. No matter how hard you fight, unless those walls are rebuilt and fortified, you will just wear yourself out and not even win.

First Step: Inspecting the damage to the wall

By night I went out through the Valley Gate toward the Jackal Well and the Dung Gate, <u>examining the walls</u> of Jerusalem, _which had been broken down_, and its gates, which had been destroyed by fire.

Then I said to them, "You see the trouble we are in: Jerusalem _lies in ruins_, and its gates have been burned with fire. Come, _let us rebuild the wall_ of Jerusalem, and _we will no longer be in disgrace_." *(Nehemiah 2:13, 17)*

Workshop 3

I want you to close your eyes now as you inspect the walls of your marriage.

1. How severe is the damage?
2. What parts of the walls are broken (trust, love, respect, romance, intimacy, fun, joy, peace)?
3. How did it break? What happened?

Focus on what you did wrong and not what your husband did wrong. For instance, if the broken part of the wall is trust, look back to where it all started. When did you start losing trust in him? Why? What could you have done differently?

4. What does God's Word say about this?

These questions, as you inspect the damage to your walls, will also help you in your healing process. As you focus on yourself and what you did wrong, your issues will be exposed. This is the prerequisite to true healing.

Remember what I said in the previous chapter??? You can't be an effective Armour-Bearer if you are wounded. You need to heal. However, you don't need to be perfectly healed to start rebuilding your walls. You will have to do it simultaneously.

Those who carried materials did their work with one hand and held a weapon in the other (Nehemiah 4:17).

Second Step: Taking note of your personal strongholds, followed by your husband's strongholds

Workshop 4

Create two columns: one for you; one for your husband. *(You do not need to let your husbands know about this. There are things that you have to keep between you and the Lord first, until it is time.)* On one column, write your strongholds; on another column, write your husband's strongholds.

Do not expect to finish this in one sitting. As God reveals more to you each day, continue to fill up these columns.

One thing you need to remember in strategizing is that it requires wisdom and discretion. You do not broadcast to others what you are doing. You do not share it on social media. You keep it a secret. This is what Nehemiah did when he was investigating. Nobody knew what he was up to except for very, very few trusted people.

Through your investigation of your walls and the parts that are broken, God will begin to show you your issues. As you become more open to God's healing, He will begin to dig deeper and show you the strongholds that have been controlling you all these years. These strongholds are the very reasons why your walls are broken. Until you attack the root source, the walls will just keep falling and breaking.

Third Step: Preparing to war in the spirit

Nobody enters the battlefield unprepared. It is the kind of preparation a person does that dictates her victory or defeat. Sometimes, the enemy will just run away scared, only to return again with a stronger force. Our mindset should be only one thing: TO WIN AND TOTALLY DESTROY THE ENEMY.

Fasting is the best way to prepare for battle. This is a tried-and-tested method in the Bible. Pray on the kind of fast that God is calling you to do. You can do a one day absolute fast, a 21 day Daniel fast, a few hours of fast each day for three or more days, etc. The best fast is a 40-day fast. However, this is not for everyone, more so if your health or schedule will not allow it. There are so many varieties of fast. Pray for God's perfect will and what will work best for you.

Having a consistent time alone with God everyday is another way to prepare. David said in Psalm 27:4-6: *One thing I ask; that will I seek; that I will dwell in the house of the Lord all the days of my life, to gaze upon the beauty of His holiness and inquire in His temple...He will conceal me there when troubles come. He will hide me in His sanctuary. He will place me out of reach on a high rock. Then I will hold my head high above my enemies who surround me.*

Part of preparation is to schedule your battle. Choose a day, place, and time where you will do it. Be sure you have your list of strongholds with you. Your warfare should cover these different parts: worship, declaration of God's promises, intercession for your husband, and cutting off the heads of those strongholds.

Fourth Step: The actual day of battle

This is how my actual day of battle looks like.

I put on my prayer shawl as I enter the battlefield. I start with worship, lifting up and exalting the Father. I follow it up with declaration of His promises. These promises are Scriptures (you should have this ready, written on paper) pertaining to healing, deliverance, spiritual warfare, and everything else you are warring for in the spirit. I then put on my sackcloth and begin interceding for my husband. I act like his lawyer, pleading his case before God. I love this part because it makes me see my husband for who he really is, the way God created him. It makes me put myself in his shoes — feeling what he is feeling and thinking what he is thinking. When I intercede for my husband, God floods me with compassion for him. It is some sort of healing for me too. This intercession is followed by the actual warfare. I position myself again in worship then stand up to declare war with the devil. I command my angels, in the name of Yeshua, to guard the four corners of my house. I put on my whole armour and declare the authority that God has given me to trample on snakes and scorpions and to overcome all the power of the enemy. I cast down stronghold after stronghold, as well as demonic kings and spirits in charge of these strongholds. I take my sword and cut off the heads of these demons, in the name of Yeshua, by the power of the Holy Spirit. Finally, I see in the spiritual realm, all my enemies defeated and dead. I go back to the Father's throne and celebrate with thanksgiving and praise.

Now you see why this battle takes preparation? It is no joke. I get so exhausted and even tired for days after a warfare. Sometimes, you may even have to do it for several days, not necessarily consecutively. Again, create a strategy that will work for you.

Once you have destroyed strongholds, other issues may continue to pop up. This is God's way of showing you what may still be there that you haven't addressed. You can destroy more strongholds after your major war, without going through the same extensive process.

Destroying these strongholds is the most critical part in rebuilding your walls. Maintaining your time alone with God each day in prayer and Word will continue to rebuild your walls on the right foundation. Making sure that you use the mind of your spirit and not your flesh is another way of rebuilding and strengthening these walls. Keeping yourself uncontaminated by the world and sin is part of strengthening your walls too. Having a repentant spirit is another key.

One thing I also want you to bear in mind is that for every new journey and/or promotion, there are new enemies to conquer and defeat. This was the case with the Israelites in every journey they took, and every land they possessed. The good thing about it is that God crosses over ahead of us. He said this Himself in Deuteronomy 31. Let me quote the verses for you. The words in parenthesis are my own paraphrased words.

The Lord your God Himself will cross over ahead of you. The Lord will destroy the (enemies) living in the land. The Lord will hand over to you (the enemies) who live there and you must deal with them. Be strong and courageous! Do not be afraid and do not panic before them. For the Lord your God will personally go ahead of you. He will neither fail you nor abandon you (verses 3-6).

Another promise God gave us is in Zechariah 2:5: *For I, says the Lord, will be to her a <u>wall of fire</u> round about, and I will be the glory in the midst of her.*

Isn't that amazing? God Himself will be our wall, and not just a wall but a "wall of fire", with His glory in the midst of us. Wow!

CHAPTER 6

The King-Maker

You can't be a queen without a king. You can't have a kingdom without a king. Therefore, your role as an Armour-Bearer wife is to make sure that your husband fulfills his role as a king. You are the king-maker.

Most men of God do not realize their role as a king, and even if they do, they are oftentimes clueless as to how to fulfill this God-given task. You have to understand that if they were not raised by godly fathers, they wouldn't even know how to lead. This is why the church is full of men who lack the leadership required of a king. And this is why women have taken over. So if you have a husband who is not leading you properly, or a husband who is not even strong in God, it is because God has called you to be a king-maker. Stop looking at your husband as the problem. This is happening for your own good, for your training. Now if you have a husband who

63

is in church leadership but is not leading like Yeshua, it is because God has called you to be a king-maker as well, the way He designed kings to be.

Being a king-maker is not like being a mother, telling her sons what to do and how to do things. This is the biggest mistake wives make. We act like our husband's mothers, and oftentimes, we take the job of the Holy Spirit, trying to change them through discussion. 1 Peter 3 is very clear on this one. It says that it is through a gentle and quiet spirit that they will be won over, not through our discussion. We fulfill our role as king-makers in the spiritual realm.

Before you can be a king-maker, you have to start recognizing your husband as a "king". This may not be easy for some of you whose husbands are manipulative and controlling. However, the key to their deliverance from this spirit of control is in your hands. Let me explain this more clearly to you.

The spirit of control normally stems from the fear of being controlled. It is a defense mechanism. It is also an indicator of deeper issues of insecurity and rejection. The more a controlling person feels controlled and disrespected, the more he will exercise control.

Proverbs 16:14 says: *"The king's anger is a herald of death, and one who is wise will appease it."*

It is not fun to live with a husband who has an anger problem; yet, a wife's anger towards him will just worsen the situation. The verse above says that a wise person, or a wise wife for that matter, will pacify it.

My husband had major anger problems that I didn't know about until I was married to him. I hated it and fought it back. I rebuked it and confronted it head on. Guess what? It grew worse and stronger. It was only after God showed me the verse in 1 Peter 3 on having a "gentle and quiet spirit" that I began to realize that the only way I can overcome that spirit of anger is by keeping quiet. It was very hard!!! I had to learn and relearn it. Now I am used to it. My husband is delivered from his anger problem and will continue to be delivered unless I fight back when I sense it. I appease his anger when I keep quiet and listen.

Proverbs 16:15 explains why it is wise to appease the king's anger.

"When the king's face brightens, it means life; his favor is like the clouds that bring spring rain."

The best way to make your husband do what you want is to make him win your favor. It is not in your nagging, discussion, complaining, and even praying that you can make him change his mind about what you want. It is by winning his favor. Nobody knows your husband the way you do, next to God. Find out what pleases him and do it (for as long as it is not against the Word of God).

My husband is pleased when he sees me humble. This used to be a struggle for me because I felt like he wanted me to be humble so he can control me. That was an issue I had inside of me – a stronghold that God had to deal with. My fear of being controlled made me scared to humble myself and submit to my husband. Of course God didn't let me get away with that. He humbled me and I had no choice. My humility made my husband love me more.

When you win the favor of your husband, no woman can take him away from you. He will be the best husband for you, and will give you almost anything you want (just be sure that what you want is also what God wants).

Remember Queen Esther? She won the favor of the king, her husband, and saved her entire people as a result. I will have more of Esther's story in the next chapter.

Recognizing and treating your husband as a king is the beginning of your being a king-maker. You can't be a king-maker unless you are a queen; thus, start acting like one. Be a Queen Esther who submits to her king, and not a Queen Vashti who refused to submit and was therefore ousted.

So are you ready to be a king-maker? If you are, the first step is for you to arise, just like Deborah.

The rulers ceased in Isra'el, they ceased, until you arose, D'vorah, arose a mother in Isra'el (Judges 5:7, Jewish Bible).

Deliverance took place when Deborah arose.

The people of Isra'el cried out to ADONAI, because he had 900 iron chariots, and for twenty years he cruelly oppressed the people of Isra'el. Now D'vorah, a woman and a prophet, the wife of Lapidot, was judging Isra'el at that time. She used to sit under D'vorah's Palm between Ramah and Beit-El, in the hills of Efrayim; and the people of Isra'el would come to her for judgment. She sent for Barak the son of Avino'am, from Kedesh in Naftali, and said to him: "ADONAI has given you this order: 'Go, march to Mount Tavor, and take with you 10,000 men from the people of Naftali and Z'vulun. I will cause Sisra, the commander of Yavin's army, to encounter you at the Kishon River with his chariots and troops; and I will hand him over to you.'" Barak answered her: "If you go with me, I'll go; but if you won't go with me, I won't go." She replied, "Yes, I will gladly go with you; but the way you are doing it will bring you

no glory; because ADONAI will hand Sisra over to a woman."
(Judges 4:3-9)

Deborah relayed the message to Barak and instructed him to go. Barak, however, didn't want to go without her, so she warned him: "I will gladly go with you but the way you are doing it will bring you no glory." In short, it will not make him the king and leader that God intended him to be.

My fellow wives, this is where we fail most of the time. We see our husbands as not doing their part as our leaders and kings and so we take over, thinking it is our job. I have heard countless wives say, "My husband is not in ministry but I am. I am not going to let him stop me from doing what God has called me to do." In fact, one lady apostle I met in the past told me to fulfill the calling God has given me before I was married because that is my true calling. That is a lie!!! God gave the vision to Adam first before He even created Eve. She was called a "help-meet" for the very purpose of helping her husband fulfill the vision that God has given him. Whatever God has given you as a calling and ministry before you were married is meant to support the vision that God has given your husband. And if he has not discovered this vision yet, your role is to lead him to that vision, in the spirit.

Once you take over, you will kill and destroy your husband's kingdom, which is yours too.

Workshop 4

1. What was the vision God gave you before you were married? If you are not very sure about this, answer the next sub questions.
   a. What ministry were you more inclined to fit in when you were single (teaching/preaching, children, music, sick people, prison, etc.)?
   b. What were your gifts and talents?
   c. What were the things that moved you to compassion?
2. What is your husband's vision? If he doesn't know what his vision is, and you don't know as well, answer the following sub questions.
   a. What are your husband's strengths? What is he good at?
   b. What is his personality?
   c. What about "being in God" does he enjoy the most?
   d. Is he a part of any ministry?
   e. What does he love to do for God?
   f. What is his line of work?

Your answers to these questions will help you formulate your vision, as well as your husband's vision. Think about how your visions coincide. Think about how you can help him see or fulfill his vision. Keep all these to yourself. You don't have to discuss it with him … not yet. Let God handle that part.

The second and further steps to being the king-maker are in this Scripture below.

Elisha the prophet summoned one of the guild prophets and said to him, "Prepare for traveling, take this flask of oil in your hand and go to Ramot-Gil'ad. When you get there, look for Yehu the son of Y'hoshafat, the son of Nimshi. Enter, have him step away from his companions, and take him to <u>an inside room</u>. Then take the flask of oil, pour it on his head, and say, 'This is what ADONAI says: "I have anointed you king over Isra'el."' After that, open the door; and get away from there as fast as you can."

So the young prophet left for Ramot-Gil'ad. When he arrived, he found the senior army officers sitting there. He said, "<u>I have a message for you</u>, commander." Yehu asked, "For which one of us?" "For you, commander," he said. Yehu <u>got up</u> and <u>went into the house</u>. Then the prophet <u>poured the oil on his head</u> and said to him, "This is what ADONAI the God of Isra'el *says: 'I have <u>anointed</u> you king over the people of ADONAI, over Isra'el. You will <u>attack</u> the house of Ach'av your master, so that I can <u>avenge</u> the blood of my servants the prophets and of all the servants ofADONAI, blood shed by Izevel (2 Kings 9:1-7, Complete Jewish Bible).*

Let me explain each underlined word to you in reference to the steps involved.

An Inside Room

The inside room is your prayer closet where all your battles are fought and won. This is also where God will give you the direction and instructions. This is where you get strengthened, where you take refuge, where you are comforted, when you run for help. You can't be an Armour-Bearer wife without having everyday quiet time alone with the Father. This is a prerequisite. You can't expect to win your battles if you just go to your inside room every other day or once a week or when you have time. You need to find time each day and stick to it, no matter what!

I have a message for you

This book is your message. God is speaking to you, right now, which is the reason why you are even reading this. I am a vessel relaying the message.

Got Up

Jehu got up! He made the decision to hear the message and listen to it. Without this decision, nothing will happen.

Went into the house

Getting up means going into the inner house, the inside room, your prayer closet, and listening more to what God has to say.

Poured oil on his head

Only then will God pour His oil on your head. The oil represents the anointing, God's unction, His calling. It is sealing the deal for you, that He has chosen you to be your husband's king-maker, and that He has equipped you with everything you need to do this. Do you realize why the oil will be poured on your head? Because the head is where the mind is, and where everything will begin. Remember, the mind is the battlefield!

I have anointed you

Finally, you are anointed!

Attack

After your anointing comes the battle you have to fight in the spiritual realm. I presented all these in the previous chapters. Go back to them if need be. You have to be aware of all issues, strongholds, and demonic kings that are hindering your husband from being the king. You also have to be aware of your own issues, strongholds, and demonic kings. Remember, the devil does not want your husband to be the king, more so you being the king-maker. He will do everything to stop you at this point. Guess what? Once you have made the decision to be king-maker, no devil will be able to stop you.

Workshop 5

1. Make an inventory of your husband's strengths and weaknesses as a leader. Ask the Holy Spirit to guide you. Do not just rely on your own judgments. Seeing his strengths is also a great way of seeing him from God's perspective.

2. Study the lives of godly kings and leaders in the Bible: Abraham, Isaac, Jacob, Moses, Joshua, Joseph, David, and of course Yeshua. Study their strengths and victories, weaknesses and downfall. Compare these traits to that of your husband's.

3. Make an inventory for yourself too, in relation to your being a king-maker. Compare yourself to Sarah, Rebecca, Rachel, Zipporah, and even Bathsheba (there was something about her too that made David a better king).

Once you have carefully made an inventory (God may continue to reveal more to you as you spend more time in the "inner house" or "inside room"), fight the spirits and demonic kings attached to your husband's (and your own) issues and strongholds. Do not expect to win the battle overnight. In fact, you will continue to protect your husband in the spiritual realm, even after he himself is anointed king.

Avenge

Avenge means revenge, vindication, recompense. The only way God can bring back to you everything that the devil has stolen from your kingdom is for you to attack your enemies in the spiritual realm. Avenge comes after attack. Attack comes after you are anointed. The anointing happens when you get up and enter the inner house.

So stop complaining that your husband is not leading you or that he is not fulfilling his role as your leader and king. Be the king-maker that God called you to be ... otherwise, you have no right to even claim to be a queen.

Lisa Maki

CHAPTER 7

Your Calling, Your Vision

Y our calling is your purpose. It is part of the blueprint that came when you were born. It is bigger than being a wife and mother; much bigger than being an Armour-Bearer wife.

Proverbs 29:18 says: "Where there is no vision, the people perish." If you have not discovered your vision yet, it is not too late. I will help direct you to it. If you already knew your vision but got sidetracked because of your marriage, let me help redirect you to it. Women who have no vision are easily swayed and influenced. They are the women that 2 Timothy 3:6-7 refer to.

For among them are those who worm their way into homes and captivate morally weak and spiritually-dwarfed women weighed down by [the burden of their] sins, easily swayed by various impulses, always learning and listening to anybody who will teach them, but never able to come to the knowledge of the truth.

These women are called "spiritually-dwarfed" by the Amplified version. They are easily swayed by various impulses. In short, they are highly emotional and are controlled by their emotions. These are the types of women the Bible warns against – the types of women who will be very prevalent during the last days. These are the women who are out there to take your husbands from you … women who wouldn't mind being your husband's "other wife" … women who don't even see anything wrong with being with married men. These women were referred to as spiritual dwarfs because they believe they are "spiritual". They claim to be "saved".

On the other hand, this woman can be you too – *weighed down by the burden of their sins … easily swayed by various impulses.* If you don't realize your bigger calling within and outside of your marriage, your marital trials will weigh you down and will make you angry and bitter. Anger and bitterness is a sin against God. As a result, you will be very emotional … easily swayed by your feelings. This is what walking in the flesh is about.

Wives who do not have a vision rely on their husbands for fulfillment and affirmation. Even their Christianity leaves them empty because there is no purpose for their faith at all. Going to church is not a vision. Being in the worship team is not a vision. Doing outreach is not a vision. All these are just activities that can give you something to do for God. A vision is bigger than these things.

Taking care of your kids is not a vision. Serving your husband is not a vision. Cleaning your house is not a vision. All these are just responsibilities that come with being a wife and mother.

Workshop 6

This workshop will help you identify your vision or rekindle your vision.

1. What did I love to do as a child?
2. What did I love to do as a teenager?
3. What did I love to do as an adult?

Establish a pattern here and see what remained common and the same from childhood to adulthood. Do not just focus on the activity such as "writing" or "drawing" but what it is you loved about it, such as "being with people", "helping others", etc.

4. What are my strengths when it comes to my character and personality?

5. What am I good at when it comes to my talents and abilities?

6. What moves me to compassion?

7. What fires me up as a Christian?

8. What type of advice do people normally ask from me?

9. If I have money to spend to set up a ministry, what will it be?

10. What do I want to change about my family, my community, my church, my country, the world?

11. Who are the type of people who like me? What type of people are drawn to me? Who are the type of people I have great influence on?

12. What types of problems have I encountered over and over again in my life?

Your answers to each question are like pieces of a jigsaw puzzle that will form your vision. You will be surprised how you will see it clearly as you put the pieces together.

Everything you need to fulfill this vision is already in you. Every experience you've had is part of what you need for this vision. Every hurt and pain forms part of the piece of the puzzle.

Your marriage is not the vision in itself but a part of the vision. The same thing applies to motherhood, or your job, or even your position in ministry. Being a preacher is not a vision but the means to fulfill the vision.

My vision is to reach out to hurting women from all walks of life, help them heal from their wounds, and empower them to fulfill their vision through writing or preaching.

My being a wife and all the trials that go with it are necessary for me to help women heal. How can I minister to a woman whose husband is unfaithful if I haven't experienced something similar to that? If I don't heal from my own wounds, how can I help other women with that? My strength to overcome my trials comes from God and from knowing that if I overcome, then I can help women overcome too.

My job as a professional writer harnesses the means to fulfill my vision through writing. This job also allows me to meet other women who God may use me for.

Are you seeing more clearly now? When you have a vision, you will see the bigger picture of why you are going through what you are going through.

Being an Armour-Bearer wife is not the vision in itself. It is necessary so you can overcome the hindrances to your vision; so you can be strengthened; so you can strengthen other women; so you can be more effective in your vision.

Marriage is not the end in itself but the means to an end.

Your marriage is not God's ultimate plan for you. It is the means to His ultimate plan. His ultimate plan is the vision that He has given you. The reason you are married is because your marriage is a necessary ingredient to your calling or vision. This is why the devil does not even want you to know what your vision is. He wants you to leave that marriage so that your vision will not be fulfilled.

Let us look at the story of Queen Esther to better understand what I am telling you. Esther prepared and trained for her wife/queen duties to win the approval of the king.

Before each young woman was taken to the king's bed, she was given the prescribed twelve months of beauty treatments—six months with oil of myrrh, followed by six months with special perfumes and ointments. When it was time for her to go to the king's palace, she was given her choice of whatever clothing or jewelry she wanted to take from the harem. That evening she was taken to the king's private rooms, and the next morning she was brought to the second harem, where the king's wives lived. There she would be under the care of Shaashgaz, the king's eunuch in charge of the concubines. She would never go to the king again unless he had especially enjoyed her and requested her by name (Esther 2:12-14).

When it was Esther's turn to go to the king, she accepted the advice of Hegai, the eunuch in charge of the harem. She asked for nothing except what he suggested, and she was admired by everyone who saw her.

Esther was taken to King Xerxes at the royal palace in early winter of the seventh year of his reign. And the king loved Esther more than any of the other young women. He was so delighted with her that he set the royal crown on her head and declared her queen instead of Vashti. To celebrate the occasion, he gave a great banquet in Esther's honor for all his nobles and officials, declaring a public holiday for the provinces and giving generous gifts to everyone (Esther 2:15-18).

Did the story end here? Not at all! Was Esther's coronation as Queen the culmination of the story? No! The marriage and her coronation as Queen was the means to an end, not the end in itself. What was the ultimate vision? Let's continue reading.

When Haman saw that Mordecai would not bow down or show him respect, he was filled with rage. He had learned of Mordecai's nationality, so he decided it was not enough to lay hands on Mordecai alone. Instead, he looked for a way to destroy all the Jews throughout the entire empire of Xerxes.

So in the month of April, during the twelfth year of King Xerxes' reign, lots were cast in Haman's presence (the lots were called purim) to determine the best day and month to take action. And the day selected was March 7, nearly a year later.

Then Haman approached King Xerxes and said, "There is a certain race of people scattered through all the provinces of your empire who keep themselves separate from everyone else. Their laws are different from those of any other people, and they refuse to obey the laws of the king. So it is not in the king's interest to let them live. If it please the king, issue a decree that they be destroyed, and I will give 10,000 large sacks of silver to the government administrators to be deposited in the royal treasury."

The king agreed, confirming his decision by removing his signet ring from his finger and giving it to Haman son of Hammedatha the Agagite, the enemy of the Jews. The king said,

The ArmourBearer Wife

"The money and the people are both yours to do with as you see fit." (Esther 3:5-11)

Did Esther know that this was going to happen? Did she know that this was the bigger purpose of her marriage? Did Mordecai, Esther's uncle, (who was responsible for her being one of the candidates for the position of Queen) know that this was going to happen? The answer is NO to all the questions. Only God knew.

You are in your marriage for a reason you don't even understand – not until you start seeing the bigger picture. And once you see the bigger picture, what are you going to do?

How did Esther see the bigger picture and what did she do?

When Mordecai learned about all that had been done, he tore his clothes, put on burlap and ashes, and went out into the city, crying with a loud and bitter wail. He went as far as the gate of the palace, for no one was allowed to enter the palace gate while wearing clothes of mourning. And as news of the king's decree reached all the provinces, there was great mourning among the Jews. They fasted, wept, and wailed, and many people lay in burlap and ashes.

When Queen Esther's maids and eunuchs came and told her about Mordecai, she was deeply distressed. She sent clothing to him to replace the burlap, but he refused it. Then Esther sent for Hathach, one of the king's eunuchs who had been appointed as her attendant. She ordered him to go to Mordecai and find out what was troubling him and why he was in mourning. So Hathach went out to Mordecai in the square in front of the palace gate.

Mordecai told him the whole story, including the exact amount of money Haman had promised to pay into the royal treasury for the destruction of the Jews. Mordecai gave Hathach a copy of the decree issued in Susa that called for the death of all Jews. He asked Hathach to show it to Esther and explain the situation to her. He also asked Hathach to direct her to go to the king to beg for mercy and plead for her people. So Hathach returned to Esther with Mordecai's message.

Then Esther told Hathach to go back and relay this message to Mordecai: "All the king's officials and even the people in the provinces know that anyone who appears before the king in his inner court without being invited is doomed to die unless the king holds out his gold scepter. And the king has not called for me to come to him for thirty days." So Hathach gave Esther's message to Mordecai. (Esther 4:1-12)

Esther thought that what Mordecai was asking for was impossible. At this point, she has not realized her bigger purpose on why she is even the Queen. It was after Mordecai said what he said that everything changed for Esther.

Mordecai sent this reply to Esther: *"Don't think for a moment that because you're in the palace you will escape when all other Jews are killed. If you keep quiet at a time like this, deliverance and relief for the Jews will arise from some other place, but you and your relatives will die. Who knows if perhaps you were made queen for just such a time as this?" (Esther 4:13-15)*

Those were the words that woke Esther up. *Who knows if perhaps you were made queen for just such a time as this?*

If I were to paraphrase this for you, it will say, *"Who knows if perhaps you were made the wife of your husband for just such a time as this?"*

Then Esther sent this reply to Mordecai: *"Go and gather together all the Jews of Susa and fast for me. Do not eat or drink for three days, night or day. My maids and I will do the same. And then, though it is against the law, I will go in to see the king. If I must die, I must die." So Mordecai went away and did everything as Esther had ordered him. (Esther 4:16-17)*

Finally ... Esther's eyes were opened. She finally understood what her purpose was – that it was more than just being the wife to the king ... that it was more than just being the Queen of the land. Her purpose was to save the Jews for that specific time. When she finally had her realization, she was ready to conquer. *"If I die, I must die."*

So you see, marriage is not the end in itself but the means to an end. You are the wife of your husband for a reason greater than just to be loved and taken care of. You are going through your hurts and trials for a reason greater than just your husband hurting you. You have to deal with a cheating husband for a reason greater than just him cheating on you. All the problems you see are just superficial, yet they are necessary for the fulfillment of your vision. Ask God to open your eyes the way He did to Esther. Ask Him to show you His bigger plan for you. Ask Him to give you the strength to do whatever it takes to fulfill His vision for you.

CHAPTER 8

The Process

God is a God of process. He is after quality results where every step is meant to produce a greater outcome; but only when we surrender to Him and what He is trying to do.

No wife really understands the bigger purpose of her calling until she goes through a process that leads to her realization ... just like how Esther realized her calling. Perhaps some of you already knew your vision even before you got married; yet you didn't fully understand the greater vision and why your marriage is a part of it.

I knew my vision prior to my marriage. I even had a vision statement. I also knew that my marriage was necessary to complete that vision. What I saw in my mind was the ideal scenario: a husband and wife minister traveling the world, writing books, and preaching to a big congregation. What I didn't see was a wife having to give up her ministry, having to take care of her husband's grandmother, having to deal with a husband who still had a lot of issues from his past, and having to deal with her own issues that she thought was already long gone. What I didn't realize was that the vision that God gave me would be put aside first for several reasons: to help my husband discover and even rediscover his vision; to heal and purge me and my husband from all our deep-seated issues; to humble me; to strengthen me; to train me; and to kill my old self … the self that was getting in the way of what God was doing.

"Verily, verily, I say unto you, Except a corn of wheat fall into the ground and die, it abideth alone: but if it die, it bringeth forth much fruit." (John 12:24)

God wanted my vision to die – not the vision that He gave me, but the way I understood and formulated the vision in my mind.

All of us have preconceived notions of things that we brought with us from our past. I was a corporate person in the world, before I got saved. My mind was programmed with that type of programming – professionalism, organization, efficiency, precision. All these was good; in fact, very good. Yet, it made me take control of my situation. I made things happen and nobody could stop me. I had a vision and I was determined to make it happen, no matter what.

The Holy Spirit could not move freely because I was the one in control. God had to kill the "me" who was trying to control. He did this through a series of trials, humbling experiences, and stripping off. Of course I didn't know what was going on when it was happening. I was crying out to God, binding spirits, and wanting to run away from my marriage. Since He didn't allow me to go anywhere, I had no choice but to find solutions to my problems; only this time, I had no control over anything but myself.

Jeremiah 29:11-14 gives us a perfect description of this process. The Amplified Bible explains it more clearly.

For I know the plans and thoughts that I have for you,' says the Lord, 'plans for peace and well-being and not for disaster to give you a future and a hope. Then you will call on Me and you will come and pray to Me, and I will hear [your voice] and I will listen to you. Then [with a deep longing] you will seek Me and require Me [as a vital necessity] and [you will] find Me when you search for Me with all your heart. I will be found by you,' says the Lord, 'and I will restore your fortunes and I will [free you and] gather you from all the nations and from all the places where I have driven you,' says the Lord, 'and

I will bring you back to the place from where I sent you into exile.'

God declares the end from the beginning, as you will notice in the previous Scripture. I will reverse it for you, to show you where it all starts.

1. The exile
2. Realization ... seeking God with deep longing
3. Calling on God, coming to Him, and praying to Him
4. God will hear and will listen
5. Plans being fulfilled

See how the process goes? It all starts with a trial ... followed by a realization that we need God ... then the desperation for Him ... then the "cry" to Him ... then His answer ... finally, the fulfillment of His perfect plan for us. Isn't this the same process we went through prior to being saved and then getting saved? This is the same process that we will go through over and over again in every season of promotion. Honestly, if you have been in this walk for a while now, you should be an expert in this. Unfortunately, we keep forgetting, which is why God is very quick to remind us.

Just as labor pains make the mother push harder, every trial is meant to strengthen us to push harder towards the birthing of a new season. Every trial we overcome and learn from catapults us to the next level, closer to the fulfillment of the vision that God has given us. Remember that this walk is not just about gaining victory, but gaining strength from each trial towards the next victory.

Our past revisited

Set up for yourselves highway markers, make for yourselves guideposts; turn your thoughts and attention to the way by which you went [into exile]. Retrace your steps ... (Jeremiah 31:21)

Do you realize what this verse means in relation to the previous verse I shared in Jeremiah 29:14? In this previous verse God said, "I will bring you back to the place from where I sent you into exile." In the verse above, God is explaining how He will bring you back from exile – to "turn your thoughts and attention to the way by which you went".

Though the Bible instructs us to "forget the things that are behind us", this is referring more to "not dwelling on our past". God's instruction to "retrace our steps" refers to revisiting our past so we can see where our issues come from, and be totally healed and delivered from these. This is what you did in the workshops in this book.

CHAPTER 9

The Release

One of the items in Jesus' Mission Statement is to set the captives free. God is in the deliverance business, not the capturing business. He desires that we be released from our bondages, issues, sins, and all other factors that hinder us from fulfilling the vision that He has given us. This is God's ultimate goal for our trials.

Hebrews 12:10 says that God disciplines us in a way that provides genuine benefit to us and enables us to share in His holiness. Verse 14 says that without holiness no one will see the Lord. The very essence of the vision that God gave you is summed up in the Great Commission – to preach the Gospel and make disciples of others. This is the macro vision that all of us share. The micro vision is what we have individually, based on the gifts that God has endowed us with, and the experiences we've been through. In short, our vision is about reaching out to others and bringing them to the

Lord. How can they see the Lord in us and what we are doing if we don't share in God's holiness?

Verse 11 of the same chapter in Hebrews says that the trials that God allows us to go through is not easy; but produces a peaceful fruit of righteousness "to those who have been trained by it".

No trainee remains in training forever. She is trained for something she is expected to do a great job in. You are going to be released from this training, in due time, once God sees that you are ready. You may ask, "but when"? "Why does it have to take a long time?"

I asked the same question and this was the answer I got from the Father straight from His Word.

I will not drive them out from before you in one year, which would cause the land to become desolate and the wild animals too many for you. I will drive them out from before you gradually, until you have increased and can take possession of the land (Exodus 23:29-30).

Let me paraphrase this for you.

I will not take away your trials quickly or you will be complacent, and the enemy will send his demons and will be too many for you. I will take away your trials gradually, until you have become strong enough to possess my promises for you ... until you have become strong enough to fulfill the vision I have given you.

Until you have become strong enough ... until you have increased – these are the main reasons why we are tried in the first place. Until we realize this, we will not move to the next level.

Let me share another Bible story with you from John 6:16-21 (Complete Jewish Bible version), to prove my point.

When evening came, his talmidim (disciples) went down to the lake, got into a boat and set out across the lake toward K'far-Nachum (Capernaum). By now it was dark, Yeshua had not yet joined them, and the sea was getting rough, because a strong wind was blowing. They had rowed three or four miles when they saw Yeshua approaching the boat, walking on the lake! They were terrified; but he said to them, "Stop being afraid, it is I." Then they were willing to take him into the boat, and instantly the boat reached the land they were heading for.

Again, if I were to paraphrase this, it would say ... *Her trials were getting more difficult, stronger than ever. She got weary and scared. However, Jesus said, "Hey, don't be afraid. It is I. I am allowing these trials for your own good." She then willingly surrendered to Him, and instantly she was released from her trials and reached her destination.*

Psalm 23:4 says exactly the same thing ... *Even though I walk through the valley of the shadow of death, I fear no evil, for You are with me; Your rod and Your staff, they comfort and console me.*

This Scripture doesn't say, "I will not walk through the valley of the shadow of death." It says, "Even though …" It doesn't say that Jesus will take us out of it but that He will be there with us. In fact it says, "Your rod and Your staff, they comfort and console me." It is the discipline of God that should comfort and console us because it means He loves us. It means that He wants us to be pleasing to Him. It means He wants us to be holy like Him.

When we finally realize this, we are ready to be released!

CHAPTER 10

Need for Maintenance

Our role as Armour-Bearer wives is perpetual. It goes on until God finally calls us home, or until God calls our husbands home. For as long as we are married, we will be our husbands' Armour-Bearers.

Whether or not you choose to fulfill this role is up to you. All I know is that when I am finally face-to-face with Jesus, I can confidently face Him, knowing that I have fulfilled my role and utilized everything He has given me to be an Armour-Bearer wife.

You are not an Armour-Bearer for just a season. You continue to be an Armour-Bearer even after you have won the battle. Every promotion entails a battle to win, which also means that every battle will require us to be the Armour-Bearer. And even if your husband rises up to the call and become the spiritual leader that He is called to be, then all the more would he need a strong Armour-Bearer.

As an Armour-Bearer, your role is not just to protect your husband but your marriage, your territory. Focusing too much on your husband will distract you. He is not your project but someone you should protect and fight for in the spiritual realm for the sake of the marriage that has been entrusted to you, and for the sake of the covenant that you made before God.

The devil hates your marriage and will do anything in his power to attack it. Of course he will attack you first, through your husband. If he weakens you, he will be able to attack the head and covering of the marriage. This is what you always have to bear in mind. This is the essence of our calling as Armour-Bearer wives.

Everything I have presented in this book is meant to open your eyes to your role as an Armour-Bearer of your husband. It is meant to sharpen the skills that you already have for fighting the spiritual battle effectively. It is meant to make you understand the deeper reasons on why you go through your trials. It is meant to make you see your vision, outside of being a wife. It is meant to make you connect your being an Armour-Bearer wife to the vision that God has given you.

I guarantee you, in the name of Jesus, that if you apply everything you learn from this book to your marriage, you will succeed. However, you need to know how to maintain it.

Focus on the Spiritual Realm

Your flesh will be tested time and time again. Obviously, we are still trapped in this physical, mortal bodies that have worldly emotions. You will feel discouraged, weary, impatient, and the easiest way to deal with it is to quit. Knowing this should help you prepare. And the best way to prepare for days like these is to spend time alone with God everyday, which I mentioned in the earlier part of this book as a prerequisite to being an Armour-Bearer wife.

Let me repeat this again and again and again: We are not warring against flesh and blood but against principalities. We are in a spiritual and not physical war, so keep your focus on the spiritual realm where the battle is won. Meditate on God's Word. Write down His promises where you can easily see it.

Lisa Maki

Do not lose sight of the reason for your trials

Every athlete has the capacity to endure whatever pain comes with her training because she knows what the pain is for. If you truly understand what your trials are for, you will be able to endure the pain and continue fighting.

Meanwhile, through trusting, you are being protected by God's power for a deliverance ready to be revealed at the Last Time. Rejoice in this, even though for a little while you may have to experience grief in various trials. Even gold is tested for genuineness by fire. The purpose of these trials is so that your trust's genuineness, which is far more valuable than perishable gold, will be judged worthy of praise, glory and honor at the revealing of Yeshua the Messiah. (1 Peter 5:5-7)

Keep trusting in God

When we get weary, impatient, angry, irritated, or whatever negative emotions it may be, we are actually losing trust in God. Each time we keep our eyes off Him we begin to sink like Peter. Whatever happens, we should be able to say these same words in *Psalm 116:10-*

11: "I will keep on trusting even when I say, "I am utterly miserable, even when, in my panic, I declare, 'Everything human is deceptive.'"

Ask God for wisdom

If any of you lacks wisdom, you should ask God, who gives generously to all without finding fault, and it will be given to you (James 1:5).

There is nothing that God will withhold from you if you desire to know the truth. He will show you the way and He will show you in detail. The only thing you need to do is ask, and have the willingness to listen, surrender, and obey. You are reading this book because I asked God for wisdom.

Learn from other Armour-Bearer wives

Where no counsel [is], the people fall: but in the multitude of counselors [there is] safety (Proverbs 11:14).

Nothing beats the experience of a person when it comes to giving counsel. When a wife has experienced betrayal from a cheating husband and has overcome, and her marriage has been restored, then this woman is much more effective to give counsel than someone who has not even experienced it. This is the beauty of surrounding yourself with fellow Armour-Bearer wives – women who do not believe in divorce ... women who will fight until the end for their husbands and marriage ... women who have been tried and tested and have overcome – these are the women who can help you succeed.

Incidentally, we have a very small private group on facebook for Armour-Bearer wives. If you are interested and believe you are qualified, email me at lisamaki23@yahoo.com. Please put "Armour-Bearer Wife" on the subject.

Share what you learn

He who refreshes others will himself be refreshed (Proverbs 11:25).

I have proven this to be true, time and time again. And it's not as if I am always the one looking for opportunities. It seems like each time I go through a trial, God sends someone to me who is going through something too. When this happens, I am forced to lay down and set aside whatever I am going through, to be there for the other person, making me almost forget my own situation.

Disciple and mentor others

"Simon, Simon, behold, Satan has demanded permission to sift you like wheat; but I have prayed for you, that your faith may not fail; and you, when once you have turned again, strengthen your brothers." (Luke 22:31-32)

No attack from the devil comes to you without God's permission. The enemy can only do so much. Once God permits the trial, He prays for you – that you will be able to endure and overcome. And just like what Jesus told Peter ... that you will pass on to others what you've learned, once you have prevailed.

One great reason why I continue to overcome is because of you. Had I given up, you wouldn't even be reading this book. It is because of you why my trials were worth going through, and why I had the determination to persevere. Without a testimony, I wouldn't be able to encourage you.

Take this same mindset and attitude with you. Think of every trial you go through as something you need to gain victory over, for the sake of the next person.

Maintain a gentle and quiet spirit

The instruction for us to have a gentle and quiet spirit is not a temporary but a permanent command. Any wife who is able to master this character is a very wise and strong woman at that.

God's commands are more for our sake than His sake. When we obey, He opens our eyes to see the wisdom behind the command. As I began to obey the "gentle and quiet spirit" instruction, no matter how difficult it was, I started to reap the benefits of peace and heightened spiritual discernment. This is not to mention the physical benefits that result from these, as well as the changes I see in my husband.

Having a gentle and quiet spirit kills any spirit of anger, arguments, fights, and any ill words spoken. It makes you see and hear clearly in the spirit, allowing you to detect what the problem really is. It exposes your husband to himself. It makes him see Jesus in you. It makes him listen.

Having a gentle and quiet spirit allows you to strategize effectively. This was the case with Daniel when King Nebuchadnezzar had a dream and no one could interpret it. He ordered the execution of all the wise men in Babylon, including Daniel and his friends. Let's look at Scriptures and see what Daniel did.

Then, choosing his words carefully, Dani'el consulted Aryokh, captain of the royal guard, who had already gone out to kill the sages of Bavel. He said to Aryokh, "Since you are the king's official, let me ask: why has the king issued such a harsh decree?" Aryokh explained the matter to Dani'el. Then Dani'el went in and asked the king to give him time to tell the king the interpretation. Dani'el went home and made the matter known to Hananyah, Misha'el and 'Azaryah, his companions; so that they could ask the God of heaven for mercy concerning this secret, and thus save Dani'el and his companions from dying along with the other sages of Bavel. Then the secret was revealed to Dani'el in a vision at night ... (Daniel 2:14-19, Complete Jewish Bible).

Daniel (1) chose his words carefully; (2) asked to be given time, which means he was never hasty or panicky; and (3) sought God for wisdom.

A gentle and quiet spirit will help you choose your words carefully, will help you stay calm, and will give you the wisdom to understand God.

Conclusion

The ruler of this world approaches. He has no power over me but I will do what the Father requires of me, so that the world will know that I love the Father (John 15:30-31).

This is Jesus talking. Listen to Him. At this time, before His crucifixion, He said that the devil, the ruler of this world is approaching him – to attack him, torment him, test him. He said that he has no power over Him. Of course!!! He is the Son of God, God Himself who created the devil.

The devil has no power over Jesus. BUT ... Again, let's listen to what He said.

But I will do what the Father requires of me...

The Father requires Jesus to submit to the trial, not to the devil. It was necessary for the bigger plan of God, and that is to save you and me.

So that the world will know that I love the Father.

It was Jesus' obedience to the perfect will of the Father that showed His love for the Father; just as God's love was proven when He sent His only begotten Son to this wicked world.

My dear sisters ... it is our obedience to God's perfect will for our marriage that the world will see how much we love our Father. And God's perfect will is His Word. And His Word for us, wives, is to submit to our husbands the way Jesus submits to Him. Submitting to our husbands is not even for them but for God. It is a test on whether or not we truly love our Father.

Jesus was asked to die for the very people He created. He was asked to suffer for the sake of those who did not and do not recognize Him. Through His death we died to our sins; through His resurrection we were healed, delivered, and transformed. Yet all these is a process that begins when we receive Jesus as our Lord and Savior.

Can you do the same thing that Jesus did ... for your husband? Can you say to yourself: *but I will do what the Father requires of me, so that the world will know that I love the Father.* If you do this, your husband will receive the healing, deliverance, and transformation that you have been praying for.

God asked Abraham to surrender Isaac before He gave us His Own Son, Jesus. He is always waiting for us to do our part, so He can do His part.

Whatever trials you are going through in your marriage, know that God has your best interest in mind. He is looking at the bigger picture, something you can't see for now but someday you will. It is necessary for your own healing, the healing of your husband, and the healing of other women who God will send your way. Through your obedience to God, you are setting the example for your entire family and the people around you.

It is all about Jesus. It is all about Jesus. It is all about Jesus.

Prayer for Salvation

I f you have not received Jesus as your personal Lord and Savior, and have not made that decision for yourself, here is a chance for you to do that. This is not some "magic words" that you say to make everything perfect. This is a sincere decision to surrender your life to Jesus – the only One who can heal and restore you, your husband, and your marriage. If you are ready, then this prayer is for you. Do not just pray it in your mind. You have to speak it out and recite it. As Romans 10:9-10 says: you have to believe in your heart, and confess with your mouth that Jesus is Lord, and you will be saved.

Jesus, I come before You, acknowledging that You are the Only One who can heal, deliver, and save me. I am sorry for waiting this long. Forgive me for all my sins. I believe in the power of your death and resurrection. I receive what You did for me. Come into my life, Lord Jesus, and be my personal Savior. I surrender to you and give you my life and my marriage. Thank You for this new life. I am now a born-again child of God. Amen!

Something just happened to you today. Mark this day because it is your spiritual birthday. Seal this born-again experience with water baptism. Go to any Christian, Bible-believing church and ask to be baptized immediately. You can also ask another Christian to baptize you. You can also email me at lisamaki23@yahoo.com. Put baptism in the subject matter and let me know where you are located so I can connect you to a church. Set aside a time each day, just you and God, in a place where you can be quiet. Use this time to pray and read the Bible. Connect with other Christian wives who can help you grow. Check all my contact information on the next page and connect with me.

CONTACT INFORMATION

Websites

Book website: armourbearerwife.weebly.com

Web magazine: godzgurlz.com

Business website: writinggift.com

Email

Personal/Business : lisamaki23@yahoo.com

Ministry: godzgurlz@live.com

Facebook

Personal: Maria-Elisa Maki

Fan Page: Fanz of God'z Gurlz Magazine

Group Page: God'z Gurlz

Business Page: Lisa Maki Professional Writing & Consulting

About the Author

 Lisa Maki has embraced the call of God in her life since she got saved in 2001. Her first ministry involvement was a volunteer work in church as Human Resources Consultant – something she was doing as a profession at that time. This was followed by a full time work as Communications Director, and Head of Women's Ministry simultaneously. From here, Lisa set up her own ministry whose main thrust is to heal hearts and transform lives. This opened doors for her to do Bible studies in corporate offices and to minister regularly to women in prison. All these she did as a single mom to two kids.

In November 2007, Lisa got married to the man who God showed her in a vision, a few months before she met him in person. After more than a year, Lisa left her country, the Philippines, to be with her husband in Washington State, USA. Together, they started the God'z Gang church – a place for those who can't find their fit in churches. Realizing that they needed to spend time for their marriage first, the couple decided to close the church building after a year of operations. They continued to do online ministry while working on their new marriage.

Lisa is currently self-employed as a Professional Writer. Her writing services include: Résumé, Business Plan, Proposal, Website Content, Editing jobs, Book Writing & Publishing Assistance, Newsletter, and other writing requirements.